# The Millennial Pedestrian

# The Millennial Pedestrian

## Poems About Walking Around in Central Park and Other Places

John Schenck

iUniverse, Inc.
New York  Lincoln  Shanghai

The Millennial Pedestrian
Poems About Walking Around in Central Park and Other Places

iUniverse books may be ordered through booksellers or by contacting:

iUniverse
2021 Pine Lake Road, Suite 100
Lincoln, NE 68512
www.iuniverse.com
1-800-Authors (1-800-288-4677)

"Open to Everything" first appeared in *Blues for Bill*, published by the University of Akron Press. The author wishes to express his appreciation to the book's editors.

Cover photograph:
"Bethesda Fountain, Spring Fog" by John Schenck

ISBN: 0-595-34013-X

Printed in the United States of America

# Contents

# Introduction

Ever since 1971, when I first moved to New York City from the suburbs, Central Park has been my back yard. For a while it was pretty ratty, as back yards go, and not a place you'd much want to visit once the sun had set.

But even then it was a brilliant and refreshing amenity. In spring it would be thronged with people, tired of winter, who'd lie out on the new grass or the warm flat rocks by the Lake or walk in the long circles the Park offers in such abundance.

By the time I started writing poetry, in 1997, the Park was being transformed into a lushly groomed garden. More people than ever came to visit. And its vistas, both human and natural, moved me in a way that was good for writing poems. The refreshed and renovated beauty of the Park helped me notice things that had always been there. The way its visitors reacted to it made me think about the way I react to my surroundings, my memories and my history. And in fact, one of my very earliest memories is of being photographed in front of a statue in the Park with my mother and father. (You'll find that memory in the poem entitled "Albert Bertel Thorvaldsen.")

While many of these poems are about walking around in New York and a few other places, they are almost all about walking around in my own mind and paying attention to what I find there. Poetry is a way of taking notes—of noticing. And then of choosing your words carefully to describe what you've seen.

*The Millennial Pedestrian* is also about my passage from my fifties into my sixties, a passage that has proved less traumatic than I had feared. Poetry helped me through that passage by making me notice that my life kept getting more interesting, not less. Apprehension can turn into appreciation; and as our elders always told us, we really do accumulate useful knowledge as we progress through life.

We just need to realize that we have it—and then figure out how to use it. For me, poetry is one way.

# Air Chime

Dark, fast rainclouds from the east
were blowing by, and the wind
carried the whistle's low moan
with them across the park.
It swooped down through the red and russet oaks,
Their fallen leaves slicking the road.

Just last Sunday morning I was startled
by this country sound,
a locomotive's moan,
as strange to hear in Central Park
as the lowing of cattle or the howl of wolves.

My childhood dreams were once
of trains of sleeping cars, of yellow windows lit,
clouds of mingling smoke and steam
streaming backward over whitened winter fields,
of polished silver rails that widened and converged
beneath steel wheels, a cone of light before
and two red lenses, snake-eyes in the night,
looking back at the dreamer.

When I was three or so my mother took me to the station,
where a big steam engine idled on a siding,
chuffing powerfully to itself.
"Come on up," the engineer called to me from his cab.
There was nothing in the world I wanted more
than to be lifted into that very substance of my dreams.
But I stayed there, by my mother.

And now, that moment found its voice in Central Park,
long after the mighty age of steam had passed,
blown there by this dank November wind,
distorted by the gusty air, by distance, and by time
into a sad, familiar ache
for a ride I was afraid to take.

# Memory Drips Like Water Through Limestone

Suddenly the guide switched on the lights,
Revealing a fantastic chamber, though perhaps
Not quite as awesome as we'd hoped or feared,
Since we'd all seen glossy color pictures of the hall
On postcards, signs and maps.

Stalactites and stalagmites rose and fell
And touched or failed to touch each other.
We all liked a formation called
"The Devil's Organ," which looked
Just like one, and "The Wedding Cake."

We heard the plink and splash of water.
We breathed dank air. And somewhere underground
That day, we lost you. Are you still down
In Pluto's Workshop, hoping that the guide will notice
That you're missing from the group?

Or are you hiding from him
As the lights in Pluto's Workshop dim,
And the voices of the visitors recede to silence,
And the darkness deprives you not of sight alone,
But of all sensation?

At the cave's remotest reaches
The water gushes in, a torrent from the rock.
Below, ebony pools, peopled by albino fish,
Lie still as metal in the great and famous halls
The tourists troop to see.

But at the cavern's mouth
Only a placid spring burbles into daylight.
We'd have had no notion that a wondrous realm
Lay just below the surface of this meadow
If it weren't for all the advertising.

We emerged without you. I was feverish,
And I lay down in the back seat,
Burning, as gaudy pictures shimmered
And reshaped themselves.
A small voice said to leave you there.

# *Manicure*

His mother held his hand in one of hers, trapping it
So she could exercise the art of manicure
On his small, reluctant nails. She had
A little leather zippered kit, with special scissors,
Emery boards, and wooden sticks for cuticles.

Because she wanted to, or felt she should,
She'd coax white moons into rising on each pink thumb
By gently pushing back the skin around the nail;
And after trimming all the nails, she'd file them smooth,
Then put the tools away, and say goodnight.

Last night, on a twilit city corner, through a fogged shop window,
He could just see inside an older man, a stranger,
Hands laid out before him at a manicurist's table,
And, her head bowed, black hair falling around her face,
The manicurist as she did his nails.

All the other patrons on this weekend night were women.
One, just leaving, shrugged into a fur. The shop lights
Shone briefly through the open door on the shimmering coat
And her rich hair as she turned her collar up
Against the winter fog and cold. A taxicab

Appeared almost before she'd raised her hand to hail it.
And in that moment, he saw through the steam of his own breath
A small suburban boy, alone with his mother,
Resentful of this fond ordeal, but enduring the entrapment,
Because he wanted to, or felt he should.
The yellow taxi pulled away, tires hissing in the wet.

# Cul-∂e-Sac

Thinking it's a pathway through the park,
People enter the cul-de-sac; but quickly
They find themselves circling
A statue of somebody
Nobody's heard of. Sometimes these strollers
Examine the statue, searching for clues
To its stolid bronze presence;
Others just shrug and move on.

It's downright serene in the cul-de-sac.
People sit on the benches surrounding the statue.
They read, eat a sandwich.
They talk to their dogs.
In shaded corners wanderers rest,
Shopping carts full of the tumbled
Remains of their lives.

The cul-de-sac's rimmed
With high Cyclone fencing preventing
The homeless, the dogs and the heedless
From leaping down into the traffic
That whizzes around us.
It's easy to enter the cul-de-sac.
The fence lets you know that
You only get out the same way you came in.

# Cop Car

"Oh God, I love New York," I think,
on an afternoon when I'm thinking
that just about everything
I've done has been wrong.

Two roller-bladers shoot along
the Park Drive, graceful as terns,
and families that would fill a bus
are picnicking in Spanish.

A 727 on its way in to LaGuardia
glides over West Side rooftops.
A little further uptown, it will bank right
and put its gear down, on final.

A couple lies,
she on top of him, comfortably kissing.
They look as if they have
all the time they need.

Ah, New York! The life
around me—distant songs
of car alarms, a guitarist's strums,
children learning how to ride a bike—

is, while not exactly consolation,
a temporary antidote for self-pity.
A blue police car sits and waits
to see if something bad will happen.

# B-17

Ungainly silver airborne thug,
built to drop down hell;
warted with ball-turrets and in no way sleek,
this glinting relic thunders overhead
flying low above the Hudson,
just about my age and no more useful.

It is grand to see it
banking oh so carefully above the Tappan Zee,
four tremendous, complicated motors
singing of a time when birds like this
could fly on two of them
and make it back to England.
Loving volunteers restored it skillfully
so that we could thrill to watch it lumber by
and envy what it did when it was young
and brave and ruthless.

## Albert Bertel Thorvaldsen
## (Danish sculptor, 1776–1844)

This enigmatic effigy—
Thorvaldsen!—
Holds a very Soviet-looking hammer,
And a chisel. He rests his left arm lightly
Right atop the head
Of a smaller female figure
He has either sculpted or enthralled.

I posed before this statue once myself, in 1945,
In a sailor suit, wooden bos'n's whistle on a string:
My father's wearing natty Army olive,
My mother's in a Sunday hat,
High heels, a flowered dress.
Graven images of men in roles, and their woman,
Also dressed to kill.

On the plinth supporting Thorvaldsen
An angel on a bronze medallion
Bears three infants heavenward.
An owl escorts them, but looks out
Sternly from its flattened metal flight
To notify us that Thorvaldsen's
Also in the angel's arms.
My father soldiers on in faded snapshots
And in my imperfect genes;
Mother is already blurred, although she lives.

One day we'll join you, Thorvaldsen,
In your Norse sky of hammered bronze
And in the summer sun our heirs
Will photograph each other at our feet.

## Circle Line

Descending from the Triboro to the FDR,
I see it from my car this time each year,
frozen foreigners huddled on deck,
snapping photos for the family
of the bridge's underside.

The Circle Line is changeless.
I'm sure the Circle Liners are the very ones
I sailed on as a Cub Scout,
and if not they're as alike
as the 1950 robin and our millennial thrush.
It *is* odd, isn't it, what makes us hope:
the robin, tugging out its worm from urban earth
and this green boat
in its destinationless orbit.

# *August Sunday Morning*

The city sleeps on quietly,
inhaling and exhaling
in the heavy coolness.
It's very still—
a passing car's a sigh
in the reading room of some great library.

This day's dawning
seems so tranquil.
And why not?
The present, after all,
is usually not the problem.
It's what we did or didn't do
last week or thirty years ago
that will create tomorrow's fix.
If only we could find a way
to let Now live longer than a nanosecond—
escort it through the intersection
of Past and Future, so it would be safe,
then join it on a shaded bench,
enjoy the unexpected quiet,
and while away the day.

# Baseball Swallow

"Hey Batter!" someone yelled,
as a swallow swished
over his cocked bat
into deep green pines
behind the screen.

In Attic times, I thought,
this bird's appearance
with two out,
the count at 3 and 2,
and a runner on second,
would have been a sign.
A base hit would have
earned an asterisk:
*divine intervention.

But we have lost our sight.
And though we see a boy, a bat,
a bird in flight,
we do not see the swallow on the wing,
the rainbow glimmer into mist.
We let the coach call all the signs:
there is no holy thing.

The batter swings away.
The bird's swift shadow
crosses home.

# Cleopatra's Needle

## I

In the tapering shadow of the obelisk

a nervy sparrow pecks around my feet.

Preening pigeons gurgle;
moms with strollers ogle shirtless runners.

The atmosphere is quartz, so crystalline
I wouldn't be surprised to see a crack appear
and craze the eye-blue sky.

The urgent push of spring is ten percent more urgent,
the green of fresh unfolded leaves more verdant
than in other springs. The throbbing pigeons,
enterprising sparrows—the luscious lurch
of life itself—glisten, as if lit by fusing nuclei.

Mute, suggestive, grittily opaque,
just behind my bench the needle rises,
as it has somewhere or other
for three thousand years, inspiring
and humbling lovers, telling tales
no longer listened to nor understood,
demonstrating that at last
all things come to a point.

## II

And when it happens—now or twelve
millennia from now—and the sky
cracks open from horizon to horizon
with a sound that might be *tuba mirum*
or the crash of broken pottery,
we may see beyond the falling shards
a needle in the swirling chaos
etched with mile-high runes
carved by delicate colossal hands
in a long-lost language
we suddenly can read.

# *January Thaw*

Sharp nose still gamely sniffing
The unresponsive air,
He falters down the park walk
Like an aged, pessimistic setter.

Another deep, regretful breath—
But in the inorganic mist no scent of life.
He remembers, or imagines,
A careful flowered garden in a distant town,
Planted by an ordinary family years ago,
Before a cold onrushing century
Raked them and their garden down.

But now, from deep within
The heap of castoff years
There comes an offering: the fertile mushroom tang
Of that green garden's springtime soil,
Where in his childhood he'd maneuvered
Armies vast and potent
Defying the daffodils
Arrayed against his cavalry's advance.

At last, behind his eyes
The patient muskets crackle out.
An icy little gust reaches through the beeches,
Shakes the last leaves off.

He starts to say something about the garden.

# March Rain

Warm as tears, a shower hoses ragged gullies in the park,
Forming deltas, photos of the Nile from orbit.
These topographical adjustments
Are winter's way of saying,
"Erosion goes on all the time.
That big black Lab peeing by the playground gate
Is making quite a canyon of his own.
These raindrops running down your cheek
Follow channels only tears could carve."

Soon the park will green again
The spidery black oak surprise itself
By waking up in April for the hundredth time.
Oh, to wake from winter, to unlearn its lessons,
To unfurl again, come into leaf, perennial,
To have a heart of oak.

# Millennial Pedestrian

Early in the century's first morning
we are its first pedestrians. Our eyes
meet quickly in a crease of air.

He's snappy, with a nice warm topcoat on,
hat and polished shoes, but carrying
a jumble of things, a section of the *Times*

jammed under one arm. He seems
unsure of where he's headed
or even why he's outdoors.

Lap dogs leashing down the curb
in search of morsels from the bagel shop
tug their owners with more purpose

than we show, wanly walking off our New
Year's headaches. I slip inside his topcoat,
underneath his hat, and join him in his head.

The *Times* today is big and thick
just like the century ahead.
The headline reads, **"1/1/00."**

He left home without reading much of it.
The 21st Century frightens him a bit—
it is the blue screen on his desk.

He can't remember now the first day he logged
on but he remembers when
his father traded in the prewar Packard

for a '49 Pontiac with Hydra-Matic,
and the family and some neighbors
climbed in for a spin in the warm

July evening. That day, he thinks,
now *that* was the millennium.
He remembers the cold night his daughter was born

and she was not a Catherine
though that was the name they'd chosen
months before

and the morning his first wife asked for a divorce
while his eyes sank deep into the swirling pattern
of the oriental rug before him

and he wonders
what he could have done
in the 20th century to be a better man in it.

I leave him in his skin, turn to see him go.
He almost is transparent, seen from here
with low bright sun behind him.

In thin January wind
last night's confetti blows by us both.

# No One on Shore
## (On the deaths of John F. Kennedy Jr. and Carolyn Bessette)

The city steams this morning
pavement damp
from nighttime fog.
On each corner cops
in hot dark blue are drinking coffee
in the breathless quiet
of vacated streets.

Soon the mourners will be joined
by embassies of state.
A vapid majesty
will descend with dreary
pomp and bustle.
The cops will sweat
to keep the curious at bay.

Falling from the sky
as life ashore advanced
in giddy ignorance;
the irresistible indifference of the sea
disturbed for just an instant.
No one on shore saw so much as a splash
no one heard a cry
no one felt a tremor as the air was parted.
Someone sipped a glass of wine
someone opened up a suitcase,
looked for shoes.
In another room the TV was on
not yet the oracle.
Someone turned it off and went to bed

to rise from rumpled bedclothes
to not sleep
to hope to waken
but to be awake
to bear the city heat
to hear the muffled thump
of helicopter blades as drumbeat
to see the blank and baffled faces fill the streets
as if in dream.

A hundred miles or more away
above the gray salt sea
three feathers float and eddy
in the air.

# The Sign

As if a column of sacramental light
fell from a lancet in a darkened nave,
this shaft of sun plunged down to city pavement.
In it twirled two mating insects, huge and gauzy.
They hovered spinning
till a gust propelled them eastward,
back to shadow.

Signs in heaven, insect flutters
voices in the traffic
cabalistic symbols on a license plate
dreams of foreign travel with a stranger
longings for just what I couldn't say:
whispers strange and indistinct and intimate
from an inconceivable, comforting Creation.
And always,
always in these inadvertent moments
visceral conviction
that I should be paying
very close attention.

The light changes
the wind shifts
I step off the curb.

# The Great Lawn

My view across and down is tightly framed by oaks.
The skyline offers just a few utopian spires,
grandly lit by evening sun.
Among the sea-green shadows
corporate softball teams correctly play,
forwarding the ball from base to base,
and on the rich new turf sprawl scattered baskers.

Soon it will be dark, but there's still time.
Sit by me and watch this flawless demonstration.
Only one dying tree, branches bare and spidery,
reminds us all else here is truly living,
accomplishing an instant
that will never be remembered

Except through you and me. For we're recording
a silent sweet hiatus in the history of the world
in which an unobtrusive peace crept in,
right after work,
and no one noticed.

## Stieglitz Takes a Picture at Sunnyside Yards

Interleaving tracks and ties,
snowy verges;
a heavy dimpled plume of steam,
bright and solid.
A solitary man inclines himself in gesture toward
the indistinct black ingot of the engine,
a line of low blurred buildings presses up behind.

Stieglitz waited on an overpass
to freeze this moment,
make it into art.
And now that moment
stirs us from a gallery wall.
The engineer, the fireman,
the switchman,
all are gone.
Their children, too, most likely.
The slow advancing locomotive's iron genes
may yet survive
in someone's dishwasher or SUV.

I wonder if my grandfather,
a Brooklynite,
ever crossed to Sunnyside
to watch this winter play of men and trains,
to see with his plain banker's eye
what Stieglitz saw.
And if he did, I would like to know
if his heart leapt.

# *Shadows*

Is any color better than the green
that's made by grass in late-day sun?
"More than just a color,
it's a state of mind,"
is how the slogan ought to go.

And as slogans go, it isn't bad;
true enough to make you think
and then agree, once you've reflected
on the times you've seen
a lawn turn warm organic emerald,
and felt yourself turn lax and sappy
with contentment.

Sure, a certain kind of sunset's awesome
in a cheesy way, and there's a blue
the sky can organize in late October
that's deep and meaningful and true
as the noblest emotion.

But for real relief, I recommend
the shadows cast by several hundred thousand
spears of grass, quaking like stroked skin
beneath the breeze's soft indulgent palm,
and blushing such a deep and fiery green.
No, it's not the sunlight—
it's the places where the sunlight doesn't fall,
the trembling darkness just behind the blades
that make me think this tended lawn
feels joy and pain.

# Quassapaug

"I'm at Quassy," mother tells me on the phone.
"It's a bit bedraggled!" She was ten
The last time she was on the lake,
And now, in wizened memory, she is there again.

A clanging streetcar stops just by the park.
In the roadside shade a shelter nestles;
On slippery wicker she rides homeward, dozing,
While the trolley, hot and festive, bustles

Up and down Connecticut's soft hills.
In unreflecting reverie, half-sleeping,
She stores away this fragrant summer fragment
Till it's needed and repays the keeping.

And now—it's time. Now the walls and nurses
Vanish like the melting April ice
On Quassapaug. Across a picnic table
Smiles a friend, a long-departed face;

And others, too, as solid as the plank
She sits on—bygone shades no more, but flesh.
The timeworn world of shifting strangers flickers;
Closer now the impatient spirits press.

# Thunderstorm: Chatham, New York

Before the rain came on
with big serious drops
as strong as coffee
it sent ahead a wave of giddy optimism
although the sky looked deathly.
So when we saw the big show coming
we sat in rockers on the porch to watch.
Stefano played *Aida* on the boombox
and the two boys wrapped themselves in sheets
then rolled down the sloping lawn
while livid lightning strobed
and Verdi filled the night.

Then there came a push of cool damp air
as if a doorway to a deep and stony cellar
had been opened
and treetops tilted eastward with the wind.
A thunderclap that split a nearby oak
announced the entrance of the storm
and when the lights went out,
Aida made her exit.

The racket of the thunder's voice,
its bumptious demonstration that it could,
indeed, knock down a tree
and douse the lights,
upstaging Verdi—
made us one with the ancients,
at the mercy of a noisy, childish god
rattling a stick along the banister
to make us pay attention.

And how we love that child.

# Elevator Dream
### For Gordon McCollum, 1940–2000

I step out on a terrace
just to get some air
but when I go back in
the hallway is too long,
the lighting lurid and unflattering
and the elevators go to wrong floors
so I can't get home.
When I see you walking toward me,
perspective plays a trick.
You grow and grow.
"I want to go to Four," I say.
You take me to a special door.
It opens up and in we go into
this outside elevator
just like the ones at the Fairmont
in San Francisco.
It's full of people.
What an interesting crowd!
We're all friends of yours, it seems.
As the elevator drops
I look you over carefully.
I am unsure of who I am just now.
You smile at me encouragingly
but your face is far, far away,
a moon floating in the elevator's
boundless nighttime sky.

When we reach Four the elevator
leans back from the building with a lurch
and we dangle by a
what? A cable? A thread?
I look around for you
but you've escaped somehow
and we're left hanging here.

Above us and below the city spins,
a geometric pinwheel grid through which
we see you walk with joy
pointing out the home of Stanford White,
the Northern Dispensary,
the Lockwood deForest residence,
Our Lady of Sorrows RC Church.

# Contrail

I look up from my book and see
a polar white diagonal
angle through a trapezoid of sky
framed by plaster, glimpsed through glass—
exhaust plume of some Boeing.
Is it the purity of blue and white—
the simple composition of the piece—
the limitless and empty sky traversed
by just one line, that stirs
this strange and sad elation?
Or is it the apparent freedom
of the plane's high passage?

The dream…the daylight dream persists
of flight as solution,
as metamorphosis to sinlessness,
a pure erasing white streak
in the window of my days.
What a fine clean dream this is.

I look again. Stratospheric wind
has whisked the thin chalk line to haze,
drifting from my window's frame.
Above the gullied grid of city life
airplanes cross the sky,
draw their ivory arrows east to west.
They are not art, these darts;
hydrocarbon residue of loud combustion,
made into an emblem
of a something missing.
Still, there was beauty in the sky today.

# Deep Thoughts

What's missing? Not a friend,
I'm sitting here with a good one.
Not atmosphere, God knows,
We're in the midst of vineyards,
Breathing rich Burgundian air.

Expectations, maybe, are too high.
I hoped we'd reach some deep
Communion, bonding over our coronas.
But the conversation's lame and fitful,
So I'm smoking much too fast.

I wonder if my friend's as bored as I am
With our lack of spark. There hasn't been
An insight uttered since we dragged
These chairs outdoors, and what's the purpose
Of a starry night in France, if not to make us brilliant?

But even though the Milky Way's a bright
Cool spill of light above us, almost casting
Shadows on the lawn, and even though
The two of us have known each other decades,
We're really trying to get acquainted here tonight.

No wonder we act awkward. Our wives, inside, asleep,
Have never needed a cigar, or foreign sky
To consummate *their* conversations.
Words flow like Beaujolais, and deep
Rapport seems to splash about them.

But circled by these grapevines, whose ancient roots
Are locked together just beneath us
In a vast and woody knot, we sit out
On this lawn, as if the stars and vines
Were not a challenge to our very souls.

So just as cats avoid a pond, we shun this gift,
And silently acknowledge to each other
That thoughts serene and grave are certainly being thought,
But that utterance, perhaps, would be too earthly
A medium in which to frame them.

Now the moon is rising, and it's getting cool.
We haven't said much, but we haven't lost much, either;
Life is long, and offers many evenings, after all.
We show no haste, but go indoors to tell our wives
About the glories of the summer sky in France.

# Evening on the Esopus River

I'm sitting on a chair-shaped rock,
smelling the smell of
water scouring round smooth stones,
watching Wally fish the river.

I almost can't see
the trailer park,
the sunlight mirrored
from the moving silver stream's
so strong, so bright.
The river's rush drowns out
the whiz of passing cars
on Route 212.

The sun has nearly set
and cool air just now moving on the leaves
will push away the heat.

Wally stands in dappled water,
holding up a nine-inch Brown.
He doesn't know that I can see him
but he holds it up.

## Photograph of a Rectangular Vase
## Illustrating Poem by Tao Qian

Of the vase, two sides are visible.
On one, a dense calligraphic cascade.
On the other, a boat floats on a lake;
a foaming waterfall, a low-flying crane,
barebranched trees—and in the boat
a small pavilion
under which two men
avoid each other's eyes
as if they had just argued
and had nothing left to say.
An oarsman steers; at the bow
a woman kneels before a stove.

The poet Tao Qian had been dead
for thirteen hundred years
when this jade-green vase
was shaped and glazed three centuries ago.

Imagine—thirteen hundred years from now
an artist reads one of my poems
and paints two pictures of it on a vase.
One replicates its antique letters
in a font once known as Times New Roman.
In the second, one man fly-casts in a river.
He has caught a fish and holds it up.
Another sits and watches
from a bank above the stream.

Three hundred more years pass.
Another poet finds a picture of this vase
and wonders
what does it mean, this scene:
one man fishing, one not?

## Conception of the Fibonacci
### for Judith Baumel

The conception of the Fibonacci

Is unique in all prosodic history.

The annals of the time do not record
"Eureka!" from the tub. But this we know:

Unlike rime royal, the sonnet or ballade,
unlike sestina, ode or villanelle,
unlike strong stress (though stress may well

have played a part) the Fibonacci
flowered in electric light. In a scratchy
sweater from Peru, the poet,
hair tied back out of her eyes, wrote
by the light of one dim Tuscan bulb,

her flat so cold the bulb itself was hearth
and lamp. Ghosts of Dante, Petrarch, Spenser
entered, found the chill unpleasant, left the Earth
once more to warm their golden-sandaled feet
on the fine sands of Elysian beaches. Outside,
a bitter wind fell from the Apennines
and the sun set early. A magpie screeched, then died,
thudding to the wet brown courtyard's center drain.

The weak bulb smoldered on, its very dearth
of heat and light a metaphor for life.
Laughter languished far beyond the boundaries
of any kind of mean, golden or otherwise.
Chilly April rain denied the spring. And what was certain?
Love would fail and poetry made no promises.
But waiting in a junction of geometry and ethics
and poetics an oasis of proportion glowed.
Its ranked infinities permitting both
the dither of emotion and the length of art,
its ratios remind her of a universal order.
As every stanza is to each succeeding one, so the poem itself
expands to hold her beating heart, the traveler, the world.

# Arts & Leisure Ghazal
## (Opening couplet by Charles Martin)

I launched my fragile paper boat on the stream,
And, for a while, I watched it float on the stream.

Fashioned from the "Arts & Leisure" section of the Times
Its show and movie ads were one big quote on the stream.

Flood-flourishing, the turgid flow besieged my craft:
Dead dogs, fallen trees, a Volvo and even a goat on the stream.

The temperature dropped as my little skiff slipped from my sight.
I shivered and started to wish for a coat on the stream.

But my boat would soon sink—newsprint's ephemeral—
Dooming my dreams of what boats might denote on the stream.

Art's long, life is short? Paper wraps glass? Water sinks paper?
I felt flummoxed, as if I'd ingested peyote on the stream.

Water rose up to my neck and I knew then the answer was poetry.
Drowning, I quickly created this ghazal I wrote on the stream.

# Greenland
## (On Sabena #568, Brussels-Newark, 6/20/98)

During the movie, I lifted the shade,
looked down,
hoped I'd glimpse something
eloquent, still and beckoning
that doubtless would have looked
exactly like a cloud
if I had seen it.
But all I saw was clouds.
Maps show us dots for towns in Greenland:
Nuuk (formerly Godthb), Qaqortoq;
sprinkled down the shore
where white becomes the polar sea's
excruciating blue.
We do not hear
from travelers to these towns.

Greenland!
Glassy gleaming isle
swelling high
atop Mercator's Arctic rim;
terminal of Fahrenheit,
ancient aviators' cryogenic tomb—
I'd like to think that
underneath your virgin's robe
there sleeps some hot dark truth of Earth.

## Lake Star

This old canoe and I
have drifted to the middle of the lake.
It's late, and I'm out here
to watch and listen
in the night
for any speck of wisdom
lake or sky or shore
may choose to share.

Constellations, inside out,
replicate themselves
in deep black water.
Two bright stars shine
dead ahead: one below
the lake's enamel skin,
the other, colder, steadier,
hangs just above
my canoe's curved bow.
They both look close enough to touch.

Now a big black dog
barking on a dock
jumps off and paddles toward
the star that quivers in the lake.
His sleek black head's reflected
over and over in the liquid gleam.
He wants to catch this sparkly floating foil
and bring it back to someone waiting on the shore.

Venus watches her remote reflection
vanish in the dog's excited jaws—
laughs, and shifts her icy gaze
to another summer lake
as Cerberus swims off.
The undevoured star
glimmers once again as ripples still
and one by one the cabin lamps
around the lake blink out.
I hear a whippoorwill.
I hear the far-off rush of wind through treetops.

# Litchfield Hills

These unassuming green and purple swells
remind me of a painting—or is it just that
hills in paintings tend to look like this?
There's more to memory than my mind's
erratic way of filing data: a landscape
may suggest a painting, or I may
awaken in an unfamiliar room,
and through an open window
a perfume may blow
and fool me into thinking
that there's someone with me,
fragrant, breathing.

I rise, go to the window,
see the moon rise, cold
over stubbled fields
rimed silver by the frost,
over the barns and houses,
over the hills, black and silent.

# On the Knowledge of Dogs

*"A dog raced through a cathedral."*—Transit of Venus by Shirley
  Hazzard

And if you saw a dog
race through a cathedral
you'd know something dire had happened:
a car had killed someone,
and not just anyone:
a family member, a close friend
or the government had just been overthrown
and blood was shed.

Once years ago in California
a friend's Dalmation ran around his house
all afternoon, barking madly.
"They do that right before an earthquake,"
said my friend, laughing.
That night the heaving coast
rocked his house off its foundation.

The ground groaned and the black sky
filled with swooning lights.
As they remade their bed
the sea nymphs' singing rose
from the cold Pacific far below.
All the dogs in Malibu
howled at something
they already knew from dreams.

# *Lycia*

I rested till grave robbers stole into the tomb,
smashed the marble box and snatched the things
I thought would stay with me forever.

My family went to great expense
to build this cliffside aerie for me when I died,
a hundred feet above the river.

For centuries I watched the seabirds wheel and dive,
saw the same old men pull flailing crabs from mud,
saw great ships set sail together out of Caunos.

And now my afterlife is this: to take my place, invisible,
among the rock doves. Stripped of all my gold,
my funeral vessel shattered, I'm untethered.

I miss my wife. I even miss my grave. I miss the schools
of fish that thronged this estuary, miss the sting of bees,
miss the misery of being a father

whose daughter loves a foreign sailor. I wish—
you cannot imagine how I wish—I had a body,
though I am free to fly above these cliffs forever.

# *Old Dreams*

Fog drapes the lake.
Oarlocks creak,
Blades thud against thick water—
The boats are hidden.

Greek fire
Scorches off the fog.
Black ships burn in silence.
No one screams.

I see you now, as dreams disturb your sleep.
Rapt in them, you're powerless
To save me from my own old dream
Of drowning in the fire.

## Anatolian Compost

Under the pasture,
ruins.
A Corinthian capital
pokes up from a field.
The farmer plows
around it.

Under the ruins,
ruins.

Peel back
the cultivated soil.
The earth here is an onion,
pungent with the tang
of history composted.
Down near the bitter core
are weapons,
bones.

Once this farm
belonged to a Greek.
Turks live here now.
The Greeks are back in Greece
plowing up the bones of Turks.

# The Antique Theater of Kas

At dusk we climb
row on row of stony seats
to view the renowned sunset of Kas.
One of us remarks upon
the wine-dark sea,
another offers to remain
until the rosy-fingered dawn.
The storyteller draws us close,
and the nervous audience is still.

Mutton drips fat
into the snapping fire,
the black ships loom up,
sails furled, on the beach.
Behind us, in the trees,
creatures breathe—we hear them.
The ocean murmurs
in a strange familiar tongue,
the sky becomes a world,
clouds continents,
and we are Homeric
in a small majestic way.

Below us in the parking lot,
the minibus silently awaits
the dark of night.

# *The Merchant*

"This rug is Eastern Anatolian, seventy years old,"
the merchant says and offers you another glass of tea.
Topographies lie heaped and gathered at your feet.
You are undone by Earth's colors,
its slubbed and bumpy texture,
its sudden nighttime blacks and dusky ochres.
Desert dunes cup jade oases,
breakers curl upon a crimson shore.

And in the warp—
the clenched and cloistered anonymity
of women telling tribal tales in wool
whose ancient meanings may have long been lost
or come to mean a different thing. The hands
of Fatima are here, birds there,
a Tree of Life;
geometry of legend into which
forgotten lives are loomed.

Stand with the light just so: there's the lake
you swam across when you were young.

# The Ruined Castle of Vysehrad

We saunter through the tumbled walls
imagining feasts in firelit halls,
plucked instruments and pipes,
a close and living deity,
an order of the universe:
of consequences.
Of lives unchanging,
of life, unchanging.
While silently, unseen green tendrils of the vines
consume the sheer smooth joinery.

# *Two Views of Chartres: November '75*

## I

Door within a door, it opens into darkness.
The organist lifts his fingers from the keys,
his closing chord engulfs us and we step inside.
Departing worshipers ignore us,
gawking tourists trying to see the space
we've come so far to see; our eyes are not
accustomed to the Gothic twilight of the nave.
The stained glass barely glimmers on this late November day.

Long before the Romans came, this place was sacred.
Dwellers in the dark green forest clearings
knew the force of an enormous will flowed from this ground
or down to Earth here.
And now we trace its old trajectories up and down
these sculpted columns. They slowly rotate as we near
the sanctuary, apexing in darkness far above us
that is firmament, not gloom.
Giddy with the spinning dance of vaulted space,
the censered air, flickering banks of votive lights,
shuffling paces of the pilgrims with their Psalters
and Michelins, murmurs from the multilingual docents,
we exit through a transept door into a dreary
Sunday afternoon that now seems full of glory.

## II

To enter *Henri IV,* a restaurant with splendid views
of Notre-Dame de Chartres, we must climb well-trodden steps
into a hushed and reverential space. The dining room
is full of formal families eating *gigot* and *poulet fermiere,*
the generations joined at table in their Sunday best.
A beacon of intention far too old and long for them to fathom
is passing through them, passing through bright glasses
of the Chateauneuf-du-Pape, passing from the ground beneath them
to the heavy sky. They hold the wine up to the light,
taste it and pronounce it good, shush their children,
banter with the waiter who has served them since the War.

Quietly, we dine. Though this is not our church, we share
in its communion. Through its windows we can see
low clouds, Notre-Dame itself,
musicians from a military band below us on the square.
They smoke and turn their collars up and watch their instruments
disappear into a bus. Soon they will also disappear
and we will walk down to the *Gare SNCF*
and disappear ourselves into the dim unwritten history of this place.

# Shoreliner

Afternoon March sun banks off the water;
A corrugating puff of wind one hundred yards offshore
Fails to break the concentration of
An alabaster swan on bronze—Narcissus,
Reflecting back upon himself in torpid loops.
Cracked ice hugs the marsh grass
Of neglected beaches.
The water holds the light
The sky has given up,
And the light is cold.

The train sweeps west,
Straight into the sun's unblinking iris,
And I know the world is ancient;
That the world is god,
That it sometimes speaks directly to us
With the voice it chooses.

# *Take One Step*

Take one step with me right through the frame
Of this small Barbizonish oil. You can do it—
Just duck down and in and
Now! A deep new breath of air,
Air like ours but laundered overnight;
An unobstructed sunlight, thick and rich,
A silence that's the sound
Air makes in grass and leaves.

Ahead, the painting's dusty road
Bends up then down and to the left,
Then disappears behind a green inviting hill.
Along the hill an orchard blooms.
The land slopes downward to a valley on our right,
And there a single train track gleams,
Hidden now and then by foliage or rising ground.

In the blurry distance where
The blue hills and the sky become the same blue
A tiny plume suggests a train may be
Serenely clattering along,
Its destination off the canvas.
Let's accept this painted invitation
And walk along the road a bit.
Now the landscape opens up:
A mile away, a Roman aqueduct
Strides across a stream, and cattle graze

Around its megalithic feet.
Umbrellas, daubs of color
Strewn about the river's edge, imply that there's
An elegant *pique-nique* we might drop in on
If we take a few more steps and leave behind
That gilded frame we entered by.

Yes, you're right of course. This may be Paradise,
But we were not invited.
The *pique-nique* may be private;
Strangers may be brusquely shooed away.
Cinders flying from the gleaming puffing little
Locomotive may ignite the golden hay
Beside the tracks; rain and lightning
May be hiding in that jocund-looking cloud.

Let's go back now to the place we started from,
Back where this small rise swells
Beside the road. I think this was the place.
Yes, here's the orchard.
But there's no gateway, suspended as it was
Above the country road.

Instead, a haze of motes hangs in the heat.
And here are sudden footprints made in dust—
And then, no trace of them.
They start and end right here,
My steps so close to yours.

—*Oh God, I'm afraid.*
—*Don't be frightened. I'll always be here with you.*

## Open to Everything
### In memory of Bill Matthews

"To the second-best writer I know,"
he scribbled on the title page of my copy of
*Blues if You Want.*
Try to imagine something more flattering.

"What it sets out to accomplish,
it does very well," he said
of an especially unambitious poem
I had just read in his workshop.

At Yale, he tooled around
in a sporty Datsun Fairlady.
Bill doted on the car, although
its name taxed his urbanity.

Despite an ostensible lankiness,
Bill was paunchy, not a graceful athlete,
but he'd play the occasional pickup game.
He moved well, for a poet.

He loved the subversive.

In his workshop the week after he died,
we tried to decide if Bill made us feel
inadequate or brilliant.
Some were awed by his intellect;
others empowered by his equable openness
to even the most awkward stanza.

In fact, he was open to everything,
and shared what he found.
*Trockenbeerenauslese*, for example.
Not so much the wine
as its Teutonic tumble of syllables.
His recipe for Pepper Shrimp
is on the menu tonight,
and though I've never quite penetrated
the mystery of Mingus,
I'm open to it.

# The Bayman

In lawless times he roved Jamaica Bay.
From brackish coves he lunged, a Dutch corsair.
Rigging lacy, sails all crazy-quilted,
crew amazed with gin. His black flag snapped
and peaceful craft took white-waked flight.

In mother's desk I found a yellowed card,
a photo of his lair—his cottage, really.
The family tree does not acknowledge him,
and though *Historic Homes of Brooklyn* shows
his little house, it claims he was no pirate:
A Bayman, eking out his living from the clam.

The Dutch arrived here
in a Reformation frame of mind,
determined to do well.
To farm, to bank, to earn.
To clam, if necessary.
The greening boughs of this old tree
must please them:
pleasant homes and careful lives,
a sturdy Dutch adherence
to the calm sea, the prosperous voyage.

Still, I dream a wild unruly ancestor
scudded into flat Jamaica Bay,
to steal fat kegs of corn, or bundled hemp or cod.
I dream the night skies shook with flames
of hulks he left to drift, to burn, to smolder,
beached on Rockaway.

# Driving in the Strong Moonlight of the 1999 Winter Solstice

We drive together all the long night
skimming through a landscape
gleaming as if made of new materials.
The moon's so silver an idea
so clean and bright and near—
the dab of dead white paint
in Rembrandt's eyes
that tells us how alive he was,
we are.

# The Coming of the Light

Her kitchen window looks out on the river
And she can see its cracked and iron surface
All winter long.
The apple orchard at the garden's foot,
Which screens the river from her in full leaf,
Now forms a scrim,
And makes the play of clouds upon the ice
A work that might be set to music.

She takes comfort from the way in which
December afternoons, when migratory mallards
Settle on the deep black patches
Just as color leaves the sky,
Slowly yield, even as the season's
Grip does not, to January's
Pale, pale wash of light.

The wind,
Which used to terrify her
When it wept and howled,
Now seems to her to be
The herald of the light,
Its birthing's rich tectonic groans
Booming up and down the river.

Her window blinks back out
Across the hillside.
If you were standing by the orchard
You could not see in,
Blinded by the sharp reflected sun.
At night she draws the curtains
So no ray of light escapes.

She peels a carrot, drinks a cup of tea.
She watches the river by herself.
The wounds and losses
She has suffered
She cannot remember;
She gives her past up to the light.

## The Gray Stripe

No ship had sailed this wide and glassy sea
Until he set out in his bark to find
A harbor or an isle of mystery.
He didn't know the ocean's moody mind
Nor did he dream that every shape and kind
Of finned and fishy monster would appear
And fill his days and sleepless nights with fear.

Becalmed: the blank sun bleached the salt-rimed deck
While right beneath it slippery shapes did slide
Touching keel and rudder, threatening wreck.
In lacquered skies the moon did nightly glide
And glisten from the agile orca's hide;
Around the bark the sharks did sleekly stalk
And disappear at dawn in billows chalk.

He heard the ocean's rending sigh
When gales arose, the iron rain's cold roar;
He saw drowned seabirds twirling from the sky.
The eyeless creatures of the ocean's floor
Were gathered underneath to scavenge for
Him—then he saw a thin gray stripe ahead.
Perhaps the land he sought—or was he dead?

# *Witnesses*

As cows and stars look on, blasé,
The festive wedding train
Rolls past neglected pastures
Beneath magenta skies.

Streaming from the smokestack
A white cloud:
A bridal gown
Upside down.

At every crossing, bells are rung
Whistles chime and
Bride and groom sublimely glide
Down wide cascading aisles.

Wide-eyed stars and moony cows
Sanctify the nuptials.
Stars by night, cows by day
Dumbly glowing, lowing.

And onward flies the train
Through clamorous stations.
Passengers pressed on narrow platforms
Shrink from its hot and swirling wind.

They glimpse through flickering windows
The wedding guests, pale and arrested,
Flutes of champagne frozen in air.
Later, days later,

On high arid prairie
The train slowly hisses its last steaming breath.
Long silence falls. In soiled exhausted silk
The wedding party disembarks
To colorless hard-hammered earth.
Writhing out to blank horizons
Dull iron rails
Are scalding cold to touch.

# *Transformations*
## *For Liz and Josh*

We are sharing in a dream,
an ancient mythic rite in which
two people are transformed—
not into frogs or trees,
but into royalty for a day.
In donning unaccustomed finery,
they slip on special powers
to make us feel anew the smooth green
shoot of love at summer's birth.

We witnesses are figures in this dream,
aswim in dreaming of our own.
Tomorrow morning all our reveries will leave
a trodden lawn, perhaps a headache,
memories still too new to quite believe,
and expectations—
dreams of transformations still to come.

In this dream we dream today,
the sole reality is love.
It brought you here
and drew us all here with you.
Here is the most real and the hardest thing
that you can do:
Take joy and care to love each other well.
And if you do
you may discover that in time
you truly are transformed
into the person you yourselves
have yearned to be.

John Schenck lives in New York City, a block from Central Park.

0-595-34013-X

Printed in the United States
28434LVS00005B/259-357